SUPERSTAR POTTY TRAINING BOOK FOR GIRLS

To my daughters, Brianna and Ava.
The sleepless nights were long and the days so tiring, but I would still do anything to keep you LITTLE.

SUPERSTAR
POTTY TRAINING
BOOK FOR GIRLS

VIOLET GIANNONE

ILLUSTRATIONS BY SIMJI PARK

ROCKRIDGE
PRESS

Meet the Potty Superstars!

You're going to be a superstar, too.

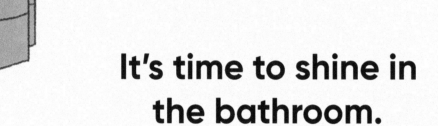

It's time to shine in
the bathroom.

You're a big kid now.
You've got this!

Say bye-bye to diapers.

Superstars use the potty!

Wow! You have your very own special potty.

It might look like this . . .

or like this!

Which one do you have?

Take a seat. Try out your Potty Power.

Great job!

**Next time your body
feels wiggly,
or your tummy
is rumbling . . .**

. . . tell a grown-up you need to use your Potty Power!

Your grown-up will help you take off your diaper and get on the potty like a superstar.

Sit all the way back.
On a taller potty, you can
dangle your legs on either side.

Relax, take a deep breath, and let your pee go into the potty.

If it's poop, you may have to lean forward and push a little. Use your Potty Power!

**Sometimes Potty Power
takes time to happen.**

**You can read, color, or
blow bubbles while you wait.**

It's okay if nothing comes out. You're still a superstar! Try again in a little while.

Sometimes accidents happen.
But superstars don't give up!
Just get back on the potty.

Now it's time to wipe!
Superstars wipe from front to
back. Your grown-up will help.

Whoosh, crash, splash!
Wave bye-bye to the water
when the toilet flushes.

There's one more super step! Wash your hands with soap and water.

You did it! Sing the "Potty Superstar" song.

I have Potty Power!
I am brave and strong.
I'm a Potty Superstar,
This is my Potty Song!

Be a superstar all day and night! At bedtime, wear your special sleeping underwear.

Wear big-kid underwear during the day.

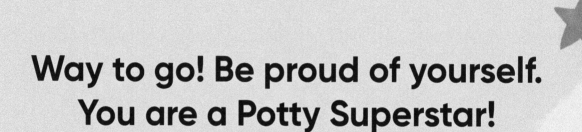

Way to go! Be proud of yourself.
You are a Potty Superstar!

ABOUT THE AUTHOR

 **Violet Giannone** is a registered nurse who specializes as a pediatric sleep and potty-training consultant. She started her sleep consulting business, Sleep, Baby, Sleep®, when her first baby was born and wasn't sleeping at night. The program quickly gained popularity as she helped thousands of families all over the world. Violet noticed that children who needed sleep training also needed help with potty training, so she launched her website, ReadyToPotty.com. She now offers a 3 Day Potty Plan™ and customized one-on-one consultations. She is also the owner and founder of the Institute of Pediatric Sleep and Parenting®, an online school where she trains and certifies others to be consultants. When she's not busy working, Violet's favorite title is Mom. She loves doing anything that involves spending time with her family.

ABOUT THE ILLUSTRATOR

Simji Park is from South Korea, currently based in the Netherlands. She loves drinking tea and wandering in the park in search of the weight of the sky. When she is not, she produces illustrations and animations.

For general information on our other products and services or to obtain technical support, please contact our Customer Care Department within the United States at (866) 744-2665, or outside the United States at (510) 253-0500.

Rockridge Press publishes its books in a variety of electronic and print formats. Some content that appears in print may not be available in electronic books, and vice versa.

Interior and Cover Designer: Jill Lee
Art Producer: Sue Bischofberger
Editor: Elizabeth Baird
Production Editor: Jenna Dutton
Production Manager: Lanore Coloprisco

Illustrations © 2022 Simji Park

Paperback ISBN: 978-1-63878-385-5
    eBook ISBN: 978-1-63878-553-8
R0

Printed in the USA
CPSIA information can be obtained
at www.ICGtesting.com
CBHW040302050324
4972CB00009B/52

9 781638 783855